Collective Biographies

SCIENTISTS OF THE ANCIENT WORLD

Margaret J. Anderson and
Karen F. Stephenson

Enslow Publishers, Inc.
40 Industrial Road   PO Box 38
Box 398   Aldershot
Berkeley Heights, NJ 07922   Hants GU12 6BP
USA   UK
            http://www.enslow.com

To Fiona

Library of Congress Cataloging-in-Publication Data

Anderson, Margaret J.
    Scientists of the Ancient World / Margaret J. Anderson and
Karen F. Stephenson.
        p. cm. — (Collective biographies)
    Includes bibliographical references and index.
    Summary: Discusses the lives and contributions of ten influential
scholars from the early years of scientific research, including
Pythagoras, Archimedes, and Pliny.
    ISBN 0-7660-1111-9
    1. Scientists—Greece—Biography—Juvenile literature.
2. Science, Ancient—Juvenile literature. [1. Scientists.
2. Science, Ancient. 3. Science—History.] I. Stephenson, Karen
F. II. Title. III Series.
Q141.A55   1999
509.2'238—dc21   98-3912
                                            CIP
                                            AC

Printed in the United States of America

10 9 8 7 6 5 4 3

Illustration Credits: Enslow Publishers, Inc., p. 22; Margaret J. Anderson,
pp. 15, 78; Marie le Glatin Keis, pp. 51, 61, 90; Reproduced from the
Collections of the Library of Congress, pp. 10, 18, 28, 36, 54, 64, 72;
Routledge, Robert. *A Popular History of Science.* London: George Routledge
and Sons, 1881, pp. 31, 39, 68, 82, 84, 93; Wheeler, Benjamin Ide.
"Alexander the Great: His Boyhood and the Assassination of Philip." *The
Century Magazine,* vol. 57, no. 1. November 1898, p. 46.

Cover Illustration: Reproduced from the Collections of the Library of
Congress.

Contents

A Note on Pronunciation

Some of the names in this book are rather long, but if you break them down into syllables, they are quite straightforward. Here is a pronunciation guide for the names of the scientists featured in this book.

Archimedes	AHR kuh MEE deez
Aristotle	AR ih STAHT uhl
Eratosthenes	ehr uh TAHS thuh neez
Galen	GAY luhn
Hippocrates	hih PAHK ruh teez
Hypatia	hih PAY shuh
Al-Khwārizmī	al KHWAR uhz mee
Pliny	PLIHN ee
Ptolemy	TAHL uh mee
Pythagoras	pih THAG uhr uhs

Introduction

The scientists of the ancient world would be amazed if they could see where all their thinking has led. We live in an age of scientific miracles. Computers do in seconds calculations that once took a lifetime. Doctors explore the human body with waves of sound. We can look at close-up pictures of Mars and Jupiter on the Internet. What would the mathematician Pythagoras make of computers? Would Hippocrates, "the Father of Medicine," be baffled by all the equipment in a modern hospital? Would Ptolemy, the stargazer, have a hard time believing that people have walked on the moon?

Pythagoras and Hippocrates were both Greeks, as were most of the other scientists in this book. Greek culture and science flourished during the five centuries immediately before the birth of Christ. The Greeks were not, however, the first or the only people in the ancient world to come up with important new scientific ideas. Some two thousand years before Greek civilization flourished, the Chinese were rearing silkworms and mastering the technology of silk making. Around the same time, the Egyptians were demonstrating a working knowledge of geometry by building the first pyramids. By the eighth century B.C., three hundred years before the Greeks, Babylonian scholars had made great advances in mathematics and astronomy. In the New World,

5

Mayan astronomers were ahead of their Greek contemporaries. They had accurate tables for predicting eclipses of the moon and for recording the path of the planet Venus. But in all those other places the work of individual scholars was not recorded, or their discoveries were credited to the ruler of the country. The Greek scientists are known by name.

In those days, scientists did not focus on only one subject, they had a wide range of interests. Mathematicians were often historians and poets. Biologists studied astronomy and even astrology and magic. But above all else, scholars were interested in philosophy. They wanted to understand the world they lived in. Before the word *science* gained its present meaning, people used the term *natural philosophy*. Aristotle is one of the most famous of the natural philosophers. His theories about the universe went unchallenged for centuries. But Aristotle was also fascinated by the animal kingdom. His *History of Animals* was the first zoology textbook. Four centuries later, Pliny's *Natural History* included information on everything from the origin of amber to what dragons like for dinner!

The Greeks were especially attracted by the abstract ideas of mathematics. Pythagoras believed that understanding numbers was the key to understanding the world. Archimedes found practical applications for mathematics. Eratosthenes used his mathematical ability to measure the size of the earth with surprising accuracy. He also drew the first realistic map of the world. Building on the Greek tradition, Hypatia of Alexandria was a distinguished mathematician at a time when few women had the chance of an education. Al-Khwārizmī earned his place in the history of science by writing the first algebra textbook and by introducing Arabic numbers to the West.

Not all of the theories proposed by the early scientists have stood the test of time. Aristotle thought that matter consisted of four natural elements: earth, water, fire, and air. Ptolemy based his work on the mistaken idea that the earth was the center of the universe. It is important, however, to remember just how different the world of these ancient scientists was from ours. Their outlook was influenced by their gods and their culture. They were limited by the tools they had to work with. Time was measured with water clocks and sundials. Distances were measured by trained walkers who counted their steps, making it a real challenge to draw an accurate map, let alone calculate the size of the world. Astronomers studied the stars without the benefit of telescopes. Biologists and doctors had no microscopes.

The lives of the scientists in the following chapters span twelve hundred years, but their influence has lasted even longer. Hippocrates was one of the first doctors to look on the treatment of illness as a science. Six centuries later, Galen continued

Hippocrates' work. Galen's medical texts were used for the next thousand years.

In our fast paced world, it is hard to grasp how slowly science progressed long ago. But the process of building and expanding on other scientists' ideas still goes on. And we are still trying to understand the world we live in.

1

Pythagoras

(c. 580–c. 500 B.C.)

Pythagoras was a religious leader, philosopher, and mathematician who lived about twenty-five hundred years ago. He and his followers believed that the key to understanding the world lay in understanding numbers. Everything could be expressed as numbers. This deep interest in numbers prepared the way for the work of later great mathematicians such as Euclid and Archimedes.

Pythagoras lived so long ago that it is impossible to be certain about the details of his life. The first biography of Pythagoras was written hundreds of years after his death. Many different accounts followed, and he became something of a legendary figure. The philosopher Iamblichus (fourth century A.D.) went so far as to claim that Pythagoras was

A 1503 drawing depicting Pythagoras (right) using an ancient counting system and Boethius using modern arithmetic.

descended from the gods.[1] Scholars generally agree that Pythagoras was born on the Greek island of Samos, near the coast of Asia Minor, around 580 B.C.[2] His father, Mnesarchos, was a foreigner who had become a Greek citizen. Mnesarchos was a successful merchant, so he could afford to give his son a well-rounded education in philosophy, physical education, and music.

Pythagoras studied under some of the greatest teachers of his time. One was the scholar Thales, who had traveled throughout the known world.[3] Thales was particularly impressed by Egypt because the Egyptians had been talented builders for centuries. By Thales' time, some of the pyramids were already two thousand years old.

Egypt had been shaped by the great Nile River and its annual floods. The river shaped not only the land and the course of agriculture but also the minds of the people. It influenced their approach to astronomy and mathematics. Astronomers kept track of the movements of certain stars throughout the year in order to predict the seasonal floods. When the floods receded, farmers had to be able to figure out where their field boundaries had been. It was important to know if they had lost land to the river so that their taxes could be reduced. In order to mark out the fields each year, the Egyptians developed the branch of mathematics we now call geometry.

As a young man, Pythagoras followed Thales' example and traveled to Egypt, where he spent many years studying geometry, astronomy, writing, and mystic religions. Pythagoras also went to the dazzling city of Babylon. The Babylonians, too, had a long tradition in astronomy and mathematics. They were the first people to use the seven-day week and the twenty-four-hour day. They had a well-developed counting system based on multiples of the number sixty. Some of our units of measurement can be traced back to the Babylonian system. For example, an hour is divided into sixty minutes, and a minute into sixty seconds. Also, there are 360 (6 × 60) degrees in a circle. The Babylonians already knew the famous geometry theorem that we all associate with Pythagoras. The Pythagorean theorem states that the square of the longest side of a right triangle is equal to the sum of the squares of the other two sides.

According to Iamblichus, Pythagoras remained in Babylon for many years, studying arithmetic and music.[4] When he finally returned home to the island of Samos, supposedly at the age of fifty-six,[5] he brought a great deal of Egyptian and Babylonian knowledge back to the Greek world. He set up his own school in the countryside near Samos, using a natural amphitheater formed by a semicircle of stone. He did not attempt to fit in with his fellow countrymen. He made his home in a cave above the city, and he preferred the foreign fashion of wearing trousers, like the Persians, instead of wearing a Greek tunic. He also wore a turban and did not cut his hair.

Pythagoras and his followers eventually decided to move to Crotona in the south of Italy, perhaps because they were being harassed by the tyrannical ruler of Samos.[6] In Crotona, Pythagoras' school became very successful. His students included both men and women, who came to be known as the Pythagoreans. They lived according to strict principles: They did not wear woolen clothing, they kept to a vegetarian and alcohol-free diet, they did not eat beans, and they shared all their worldly goods as well as their philosophical ideas. The Pythagoreans were fascinated by knowledge for its own sake.

Pythagoras' followers belonged to two different groups, the Listeners and the Mathematicians. These two groups split up after Pythagoras' death, each arguing that they were his true followers. The Listeners based their claim on the fact that they had memorized Pythagoras' exact words. They tended to be secretive about his teachings, but some of their rules have come down to us. These cover a wide range of topics, as in the following examples:

Follow the gods and restrain your tongue above all else. . . .

Speak not of Pythagorean matters without light.

Let not a swallow nest under your roof.

Be not possessed by irrepressible mirth.

Cut not your fingernails at a sacrifice. . . .

Abstain from beans. . . .

Abstain from [eating] living things.[7]

The Mathematicans argued that they were Pythagoras' true followers because they expanded on his ideas. People did not take personal credit for their work, so it is difficult to separate Pythagoras' ideas from those of the Mathematicians.

Pythagoras and his followers were the first to recognize that numbers could be odd or even. Each number had a different meaning or virtue associated with it: 4 stood for justice; 5 was associated with marriage. Ten was an important number because it is composed of the sum of the first four numbers (1 + 2 + 3 + 4 = 10). The Pythagoreans regarded 10 as holy and called it *tetractys*.

Pythagoras did his mathematical work using pebbles because numerals had not yet been invented. He found that different numbers of pebbles could best be arranged in different shapes. He called 6 and 10 triangular numbers because they can be arranged in triangles. The next triangular number is 15, and after that 21. Numbers such as 9 and 16 are square numbers. Twelve is an oblong number. Looking at numbers as arrangements of pebbles on a flat surface led to the study of geometry. Pythagoras and his followers did not study geometry for practical reasons as the Egyptians did. Instead, they studied it for its own sake and saw geometry as a way to think about the world.

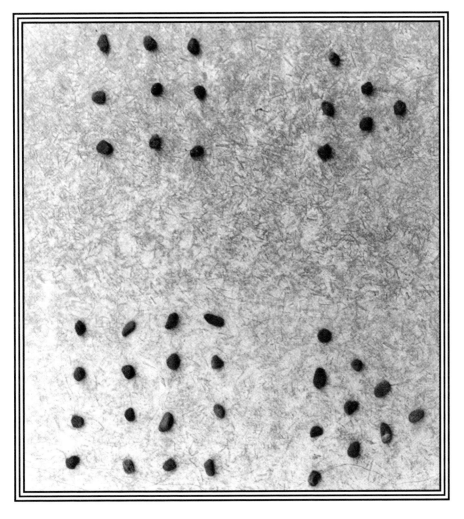

Pythagoras studied geometry using pebbles since numerals did not exist during his time.

The Pythagoreans were dismayed to find that the diagonal of a square with sides that are whole numbers is not itself a whole number. For example, the length of the diagonal of a square whose sides measure 1 unit is $\sqrt{2}$ units. We call $\sqrt{2}$ an irrational number; the Pythagoreans called it "unmentionable." They were so bothered by these unmentionable numbers that they decided to keep them secret. According to a legend, one unfortunate person who made the unmentionable numbers public was punished by the gods and died in a shipwreck.[8]

While playing an ancient stringed instrument, according to legend, Pythagoras noticed a relationship between the musical scale and the length of the vibrating string. When the length of the string was halved, it produced a note that was one octave higher. Changing the length by a ratio of 2 to 3 produced the musical interval known as the fifth. A ratio of 3 to 4 gave the interval known as the fourth. Pythagoras thought that numbers, music, and astronomy were so closely related that the movement of the planets produced music. He called this the music of the spheres.[9]

Pythagoras died around 500 B.C. Many conflicting tales exist concerning his death. In one account, a rival group set fire to the meetinghouse where the Pythagoreans were gathered during a period of unrest. Pythagoras escaped from the burning building but was caught and killed when he balked at crossing a field of beans. In another version, Pythagoras fled and later died in exile in the city of Metapontum.[10]

Although the details of Pythagoras' life and death have been obscured by time, he is an important figure in the history of science. He and his followers laid a foundation for Greek mathematics. One of the great scholars who came after him was Euclid, who lived around 300 B.C. Euclid's thirteen-volume textbook, *Elements*, contained a proof of the theorem of Pythagoras. It also tackled those unmentionable numbers that so troubled the Pythagoreans. *Elements* became the most widely used math textbook of all time. It could be found in classrooms right up to the twentieth century.

Hippocrates

2

Hippocrates
(c. 460–c. 377 B.C.)

Many medical schools still include the Hippocratic oath as part of the graduation ceremony. New doctors agree to treat patients to the best of their ability and judgment. They promise to live good lives, to be honest in their dealings with patients, and to keep confidential all that their patients tell them. This oath comes to us from Hippocrates, a Greek physician who lived in the fifth and fourth centuries B.C. He added so much to the understanding of illness and the care of the sick that he is known as the Father of Medicine.

Before the time of Hippocrates, the treatment of disease was closely tied to religion. The Greek god of healing was called Asclepius. The sick and injured were taken to temples dedicated to the god, where they took purifying baths and other treatments and slept in special dormitories. Priests, known as *Asclepiads*, acted as doctors. These doctors were deeply interested in their patients' dreams. They believed that healing could come in the form of a dream or that advice received during a dream could suggest the treatment. Patients who recovered were expected to give gifts to the temple.

Long ago, people went to doctors with different expectations from those we have today. We want to know what is wrong (a diagnosis), and we want to be cured. In ancient Greece, people were not interested in the name of their illness; they wanted to know how long the illness would last (a prognosis). Would they recover or die? They asked doctors the same questions that they would ask an oracle or a fortune-teller. A big part of the doctor's job was to forecast the course of the illness.

The doctor-priests sometimes prescribed medicines that were obtained from plants gathered by rhizomists, or root diggers. Knowledge about which plants were most beneficial had been passed down through generations, and the healing properties of those plants was regarded as a form of magic. The root diggers' work became cloaked in superstition. They believed that for some plants the magic only worked if they were gathered at night. Others had to be picked under the waxing or the waning moon. As one writer puts it, "The gathering of herbs or the digging of roots from the bosom of Mother Earth was [like] pulling hairs from the back of a sleeping tiger, a dangerous occupation unless proper precautions were observed."[1]

Late in the fifth century B.C., Hippocrates introduced a new way of looking at diseases. He no longer relied on magic or dreams or on the gods to explain their causes or their cures.

Because he lived so long ago, the details of his personal life are sketchy. The only fragment of physical description that has come down to us is that he was short.[2] He was born on the island of Cos in the southeast Aegean Sea about 460 B.C. He was named after his grandfather, who was a doctor-priest at the local temple dedicated to Asclepius, one of the foremost healing temples in Greece. Hippocrates' father, Heraclides, was also an Asclepiad. It is not surprising that, as his father's helper, Hippocrates ended up in the same career. In time, his sons, Thessalos and Dracon, and his son-in-law, Polybos, became his helpers or apprentices. They promoted his new approach to healing.

Hippocrates practiced medicine long before people knew about germs or bacteria. He believed that sickness occurred when fluids in the body were out of balance. These fluids were called humors. They were divided into four groups: blood, phlegm, yellow bile, and black bile; and they were associated with four qualities: dryness, dampness, heat, and cold. An

Hippocrates was born on the Greek island of Cos and gave medical advice to the king of Macedonia.

illness could only be cured by bringing the humors back into balance. Treatments to restore the balance of the humors included laxatives and bloodletting.

Although some of his ideas sound strange in our modern scientific world, the great contribution that Hippocrates made was to place medicine on a scientific footing. This is illustrated in a medical essay that he wrote on an illness (probably epilepsy) that was known to the Greeks as the sacred disease. Hippocrates argued that the illness is not "more divine or more sacred than any other disease, but has a natural cause, and its supposed divine origin is due to men's inexperience, and to their wonder at its peculiar character." He finishes up by saying,

> My own view is that those who first attributed a sacred character to this malady were like the magicians, purifiers, charlatans, and quacks of our own day, men who claim great piety and superior knowledge. Being at a loss and having no treatment that would help, they concealed and sheltered themselves behind superstition, and called this illness sacred, in order that their utter ignorance might not be manifest.[3]

Hippocrates was the first doctor to record case histories of the diseases that he treated. His approach was scientific and honest. He noted his failures as well as his successes. His descriptions of the symptoms of illnesses are often so accurate that doctors today can tell what the illnesses must have been. In the following passage, he was apparently writing about an outbreak of mumps:

> Many people suffered from swellings near the ears, in some cases on one side only; in others both sides were involved. Usually there was no fever, and the patient was not confined to bed. In a few cases there was slight fever. In all cases the swellings subsided without harm. . . . Boys, young men, and male adults in the prime of life were chiefly affected, and . . . those given to wrestling and gymnastics were specially liable.[4]

At that time, people did not have a complete understanding of anatomy because the ancient Greeks believed that dissecting a human body offended the gods. Doctors were, however, expected to do some surgery. With so many young men involved in athletics and in warfare, doctors needed to be good at setting broken bones and applying splints. Bandaging was an important skill when dealing with open wounds. There were, of course, no anesthetics or antiseptics, so the chance of infection was high.

Malaria was a widespread problem in ancient Greece. With malaria, periods of high fever occur at regular intervals. A good doctor would know when to expect the most dangerous or critical days and could help prepare the patient for those days. Doctors did not have thermometers to measure the patient's temperature, but they were skilled at recognizing fevers. They could tell different types of fever by examining a patient's skin, tongue, eyes, urine, and sweat. They did not, however, seem to have measured the pulse. This is surprising, considering how carefully doctors observed their patients.

Hippocrates believed in the healing power of nature. He said that a patient should be allowed to rest completely and should be put on a very light diet. He was also concerned with the patient's peace of mind. An atmosphere of cheerfulness and hope was important. He urged doctors to deal gently with their patients: "If there be an opportunity of serving one who is a stranger in financial straits, give full assistance to all such. For where there is love of man, there is also love of the art."[5]

Much of what we know about the teachings of Hippocrates is based on a collection of about sixty important texts known as the *Hippocratic Corpus.*[6] Despite the name, scholars have decided that the books were not all written by Hippocrates. They vary too much in style and content to be the work of only one author. The *Corpus,* however, provides us with a clear picture of many of the ideas that Hippocrates and his followers held about medicine. Some seem to have been written as handbooks for doctors or medical students. Others were aimed at the general public. Some are case histories of various diseases.

One of the texts of the *Corpus* that is attributed to Hippocrates himself is a book of proverbs titled *Aphorisms.* These brief sayings show that he was a man of both wisdom and humor. Some of them are still part of our everyday language. Sayings such as "Desperate diseases need desperate remedies" and "One man's meat is another man's poison" have been around for nearly twenty-five hundred years. One proverb that Hippocrates himself seems to have lived by is "Prayer indeed is good, but while calling on the gods, a man should himself lend a hand."[7]

Hippocrates was widely respected both as a doctor and as a teacher. He gave medical advice to the kings of Macedonia and Persia. The philosopher Plato wrote about a young man of Athens who traveled to Cos to learn medicine from the famous doctor Hippocrates. A generation later, Aristotle mentioned Hippocrates' greatness as a physician.

Hippocrates believed in preventive medicine. He recommended a light diet and moderate exercise. He apparently followed his own advice, because he lived to a very old age. Most sources say that he died in Larissa in 377 B.C. That would make him eighty-three years old. Other sources give the year of his death as 357 B.C., making him one hundred and three! Either way, that is a long life, especially in ancient times.

3

Aristotle

(384–322 B.C.)

Aristotle is one of the best-known scholars of ancient times. As a philosopher, he introduced ways of thinking that influenced people for two thousand years. But he was also a keen collector and list maker. He and his students classified everything from animals to manuscripts, from maps to words. If Hippocrates is the Father of Medicine, then Aristotle deserves the title Father of Biology. He was the author of *A History of Animals*, the first book on zoology. His student Theophrastus (c. 371–286 B.C.) wrote the first botany book, *An Account of Plants.*

Aristotle was born in 384 B.C. in Stagira in northern Greece. His father, Nicomachus, was a doctor at the royal court of Macedonia. Aristotle's parents died

Aristotle

while he was still a boy, and he was raised by relatives. At the age of seventeen he went to Athens to study at Plato's Academy. The philosopher Plato, who was about sixty years old at that time, had studied under Socrates. Aristotle was thus exposed to the traditions and learning of two of the world's greatest philosophers.

Before Aristotle's time, education in ancient Greece centered on music, poetry, and athletics. At the beginning of the fifth century B.C., reading and writing were added to the curriculum. About fifty years later, traveling teachers called Sophists came on the scene. They taught politics and citizenship to older students. The Sophists usually held their classes in public squares where they were highly visible and could attract new students. If interest fell away, they simply moved to another city. Plato differed from these earlier teachers because he established a permanent school in Athens. The school, called the Academy, was in a huge public gymnasium just outside the city wall. Classes were conducted as seminars, with the more learned scholars discussing ideas with those who were not as far along in their studies. Aristotle apparently stood out as a student. Plato called him Anagnostes, which means "the reader" or "the brain."[1]

Aristotle stayed at the Academy as a pupil and teacher for twenty years. He left Athens soon after Plato's death in 347 B.C. and traveled to Asia Minor, where he settled for a while in the harbor town of

Assos. He became a teacher and an adviser at the court of the ruler, Hermeias. While in Assos, Aristotle married Hermeias' niece Pythias. Aristotle and Pythias had one daughter, also named Pythias. During Aristotle's later years, Pythias died and he remarried. His second wife, Herpyllis, bore him a son, who was named Nicomachus after Aristotle's father.[2]

In 343 B.C., King Philip of Macedonia invited Aristotle to tutor his thirteen-year-old son, Alexander. Aristotle taught the prince for the next three years. The youth's schooling ended when he had to take over as regent while his father was away at war. Aristotle stayed on in Macedonia, and this turned out to be a productive period for him as a philosopher, a scientist, and a writer. He was fascinated by animals, particularly marine creatures. The sea urchin is still known as Aristotle's lantern, because he described its life history so accurately. He recognized that dolphins are air-breathing mammals and not fish. His description of the life of the honeybee was not improved upon until the eighteenth century. He observed that each hive had only one queen, though he called it the "king" or "leader."[3]

In his *History of Animals*, Aristotle described more than five hundred species. He divided animals into two main groups—"blooded" (having red blood) and "bloodless." The first group was further divided into quadrupeds (four-footed animals) that give birth to living young, marine animals that give

An 1881 drawing depicting Aristotle (on the right) with his most famous student, Alexander the Great.

birth to living young, egg-laying quadrupeds, birds, and fish. The bloodless animals were divided into subgroups that included shellfish, crabs, and insects. Setting up a system of classification was an important step in the scientific study of animals.

Aristotle recognized that humans are part of the animal kingdom. He started the *History of Animals* by describing external and internal features of the human body. Human dissection was not permitted in ancient Greece, but Aristotle described the brain, lungs, heart, and blood vessels on the basis of his dissections of lower animals.

Aristotle was not an experimental scientist. He drew general conclusions from careful observations. A good example of his scientific method can be seen in his description of the development of a chick within an egg. He incubated more than twenty eggs under several hens and then examined one egg each day. He found that "with the common hen, after three days and three nights there is the first indication of the embryo." Soon "the heart appears, like a speck of blood, in the white of the egg. This point beats and moves as though endowed with life. . . . A little afterwards the body is differentiated, at first very small and white. The head is clearly distinguished, and in it the eyes, swollen out to a great extent."[4]

Like other scholars of his time, Aristotle was interested in more than one branch of science. He studied everything from the development of a chicken's egg to the organization of the universe. He puzzled over basic questions: Why do objects fall to the ground? Why does water spread out and find its own level? Why do flames reach upward? He proposed that matter consists of a mixture of four natural elements: earth, water, fire, and air. As well as being dry or wet, hot or cold, each of these elements is heavy or light. Earth and water are heavy, with earth being the heavier of the two. Both air and fire are light, but fire is lighter than air. If these elements all existed in a pure state, earth would collect at the center of the universe with a layer of water around it, and air beyond that, and finally a layer of fire. This does not happen because all substances are a mixture of elements, but bodies are still drawn toward their natural place. Thus, heavy objects are pulled toward the center of the earth and flames burn upward.

Aristotle saw the universe as a series of spheres with the earth at the center and the stars and planets circling around it. The earth and the air above it were characterized by change—birth, growth, decay, and death on the earth, and the clouds, wind, and rain in the air. In contrast, the outer universe was unchanging. The same stars and planets had circled the earth for untold generations. Aristotle came to the conclusion that stars and planets must be composed of a different basic substance, which he called "aether."[5]

In 334 B.C., Aristotle returned to Athens, where he opened his own school. It was known as the Lyceum because the building was in a grove sacred to Apollo Lyceius, the wolf god. The climate in Athens is warm, and Aristotle liked to conduct classes outdoors. He lectured his students while walking about in the grove. This earned his students the nickname "the Peripatetics" or the walkabouts. Aristotle was an inspiring teacher, though the only description of his physical appearance is not complimentary. According to the historian Diogenes Laertius, Aristotle "spoke with a lisp, . . . his calves were slender, his eyes small and he was conspicuous by his attire, his rings and the cut of his hair."[6]

Meanwhile, Aristotle's former pupil, Alexander, was shaping history. When Philip of Macedonia was assassinated in 336 B.C., Alexander became king. He was twenty years old and only reigned for thirteen years. During that short time he managed to conquer a large part of the known world. He is remembered as Alexander the Great.

Alexander also shaped the history of science. In 332 B.C., he founded the city of Alexandria in Egypt, which soon became a flourishing center of culture and scientific thought. When he became rich and famous, the young king did not forget his old teacher. He gave money to the Lyceum and provided the school's museum with specimens of plants, animals, and rocks from distant places. This made the Lyceum very different from the Academy, which had no collections or museum. Plato, however, would not have been interested in having a museum. He dealt with abstract ideas whereas Aristotle preferred to teach from objects that his students could see and touch.

One of Aristotle's most famous students was Theophrastus, a young naturalist he had met during his travels. Theophrastus shared his great teacher's range of interests, but they did not agree on everything. Theophrastus did not include fire as one of the four natural elements. Like Aristotle, he was a great organizer and list maker. His specialty was the plant kingdom. In his *Account of Plants*, he described 550 species; some were from as far away as India.

In 323 B.C., King Alexander died of a fever. His death was followed by the breakup of his huge empire. Many people in Athens had resented the power of the Macedonians. They knew that Alexander had supplied funds to Aristotle and also that Aristotle had Macedonian connections. They trumped up charges against the great scholar, accusing him of not being mindful of the old gods. Aristotle fled to the city of Chalcis, leaving his school in the hands of Theophrastus. Within a few months, Aristotle died of a fever. Theophrastus continued Aristotle's way of teaching and guided the Lyceum wisely for the next thirty-six years.

Archimedes

Archimedes

(c. 287–212 B.C.)

Archimedes is famous for his clever inventions, for his work with levers and pulleys, and for running naked through the streets of Syracuse shouting, "Eureka! Eureka!" This is probably not the way he would have chosen to be remembered. Archimedes was a brilliant mathematician. Mathematical ability is what he, himself, thought was important, and it is why his peers admired him.

Archimedes was the son of a Greek astronomer named Pheidias. He was born about 287 B.C. in the seaport city of Syracuse in Sicily, an island in the Mediterranean Sea. During the third century B.C., Sicily was caught between two warring neighbors. Rome, the capital of Italy, was to the north, and the powerful city of Carthage in Africa lay to the south.

The series of wars between these two rival cities were known as the Punic Wars. At the outbreak of the First Punic War, King Hiero I of Syracuse allied himself with Carthage, but he later agreed to pay tribute to Rome in exchange for protection.

Much of what is known about Archimedes was recorded by historians writing about the wars and politics of the period. They were only interested in the practical side of science. They recorded colorful stories about the great man's miraculous inventions but said little about his mathematical theories. They described him as an eccentric genius who became so lost in his studies that he forgot to eat, to sleep, or to bathe.

As a young man, Archimedes traveled to Alexandria in Egypt, which was an important center of learning. Its library was famous throughout the civilized world. While he was there, Archimedes met some of the great scientists of his time, including the astronomer Conon and the geographer Eratosthenes.[1] Archimedes later dedicated two of his mathematical works to Eratosthenes.

During his stay in Alexandria, Archimedes invented a screw pump as a way of raising water. The pump consisted of a wooden cylinder with thin strips of wood wound around it in a spiral. This was sealed with pitch and placed inside a hollow tube. A handle at the top was turned, making the spiral rotate. When one end was placed in water at an angle, water trapped in the spiral moved upward. This invention,

A diagram of Archimedes' screw pump, which is used to raise water.

now known as the Archimedian screw, has many practical uses, including emptying the bilgewater from ships and bringing water up to fields for irrigation.

One of the most famous stories about Archimedes involves his studies of buoyancy. King Hiero had given a craftsman some gold to make into a crown. When the king received the crown, it was the correct weight, but he suspected the craftsman of stealing some of the gold and replacing it with silver. King Hiero asked Archimedes if he could prove his suspicions without destroying the crown.

Later in the day, Archimedes visited the public bathhouse. He was still thinking about the king's crown when he stepped into the bath, which was full to the brim. As he did so, some water spilled out onto the floor. Archimedes had the answer to his problem! He jumped out of the bath and ran off to tell the king the news, shouting "Eureka!" (meaning "I've found it!").[2]

When the water poured over the top of the bath, Archimedes realized that this was because he was displacing it. The bigger an object is, the more water it displaces. He reasoned that silver is lighter than gold, so a crown made from silver would be bigger than a crown made from an equal weight of pure gold. It would therefore displace more water. A crown made from a mixture of the two metals would displace less water than a crown made from an equal weight of silver and more water than a crown of pure gold.

Knowing this, Archimedes figured out the composition of the crown. He discovered the craftsman's deception and laid the foundation for the science of hydrostatics.

Archimedes became fascinated with the interaction of solids and fluids. He wrote a book called *Floating Bodies.* He also wrote extensively on other subjects, including astronomy, geometry, optics, and arithmetic. In *The Method of Mechanical Theorems,* Archimedes described his methods for solving mathematical problems. In another book, titled *Measurement of the Circle,* Archimedes calculated the relationship between the diameter of a circle and its circumference. This relationship is now known as π (pronounced "pie"). Archimedes calculated its value to be between 3 10/71 and 3 1/7. This important number is found in many equations relating to circles, spheres, and cylinders. In his longest work, called *On the Sphere and the Cylinder,* Archimedes discussed the relationship between a sphere and a cylinder of the same height and width. He also determined the calculation for the surface area of a sphere. His books provide us with a far more scholarly picture of him than historians' descriptions do.

Archimedes was interested in arithmetic as well as in geometry. In his work *The Sandreckoner,* Archimedes calculated the number of grains of sand it would take to fill the universe. This was a daunting task. The Greek number system made even simple calculations difficult, and there was no way to write very large numbers. In addition to estimating the size of the universe, he had to invent a way of writing very large numbers.

Archimedes thought about the shape of the universe as well as its size. He built a mechanical model of the solar system to show the movements of the sun, the moon, and the planets, as seen from the earth. His planetarium was so detailed that it showed the phases of the moon and its eclipses.[3]

Archimedes was also fascinated by levers and pulleys. According to legend, he impressed King Hiero by lifting a fully laden ship with compound pulleys. After accomplishing this feat, he boasted, "Give me a place to stand on, and I will move the earth."[4]

Many of Archimedes' most famous inventions were related to warfare. At the start of the Second Punic War in 218 B.C., General Hannibal of Carthage led a huge army that included thirty-seven war elephants over the Alps into Italy. In spite of this powerful threat, King Hiero remained loyal to Rome.

However, when the king died in 215 B.C., his fifteen-year-old grandson took the throne and switched sides. The Romans then attacked Syracuse, but they were not immediately successful. The city, which had good natural defenses, was made even more secure by Archimedes' inventions. He set up a series of catapults facing out to sea. According to the historian Polybius:

Archimedes had constructed artillery which could cover a whole variety of ranges, so that while the attacking ships were still at a distance he scored so many hits with his catapults and stone-throwers that he was able to cause them severe damage and harass their approach. Then, as the distance decreased and these weapons began to carry over the enemy's heads, he resorted to smaller and smaller machines, and so demoralized the Romans that their advance was brought to a standstill.[5]

Archimedes had other tricks up his sleeve. He designed immense cranes that could pick up boats and sink them. They could also drop huge boulders on them. Archimedes is credited with designing large mirrors to burn ships to ashes by focusing the sun's rays. Although this is a popular story, it is probably not true.

Since the Romans could not take Syracuse, General Marcellus decided to besiege the city instead. Two years later, when he finally launched a successful attack, Archimedes died at the hands of one of the conquering soldiers. The story has it that he was busy with a geometry problem during the invasion. While he was studying a diagram that he had drawn in the dirt, a Roman soldier came along and threatened to kill him. The old man begged him to wait until he had solved the problem, but the soldier had no mercy. Archimedes was killed in 212 B.C. at the age of seventy-five years.

The Roman historian Livy reports that General Marcellus was very distressed when he heard about Archimedes' death. He writes that Marcellus "had him properly buried and his relatives inquired for."[6] A diagram of a cylinder and a sphere was engraved on his tombstone, a fitting memorial for a great mathematical genius.

5

Eratosthenes

(c. 276–c. 194 B.C.)

Eratosthenes was a scholar with many interests. He wrote everything from comic plays and poetry to astronomy books and math problems. His great love, however, was geography. This is even reflected in his poetry. After describing the ascent of the god Hermes into the heavens, he tells how the different climate zones on earth would look from above.[1] His most famous accomplishment is that he figured out a way to measure the size of the earth. His result was surprisingly accurate.

Even the other ancient Greek scholars, who all studied a wide variety of subjects, looked on Eratosthenes as a jack-of-all-trades. Some of them also considered him a master of none. One of the nicknames they gave him was Beta, the second letter

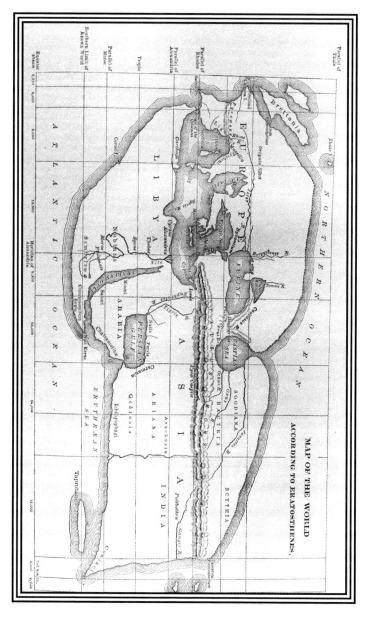

Eratosthenes' map of the world.

of the Greek alphabet.[2] Apparently they did not think he rated an Alpha. They also called him Pentathlos, the name given to athletes who did well in the pentathlon in the Olympic Games. In Eratosthenes' case this did not refer to his athletic ability but to his many interests.[3] Despite their less-than-glowing opinion of him, Eratosthenes was brilliantly ahead of his time.

Eratosthenes was born around 276 B.C. in Libya in the city of Cyrene, which is now called Shahhat. His father's name was Aglaos. Eratosthenes spent his life in three of the greatest cities of the ancient Greek world—Cyrene, Athens, and Alexandria. He began his education in his home city of Cyrene with the scholar Callimachus, who taught him poetry and grammar. After that Eratosthenes studied mathematics and science in Athens at the Lyceum, the school founded by Aristotle almost one hundred years earlier. In 255 B.C., King Ptolemy III of Alexandria invited Eratosthenes to come to Alexandria to act as tutor to his son. Eratosthenes was given a post at the great library, where his old teacher Callimachus also worked.[4]

Alexandria attracted many of the best scholars in the world. The Alexandrian kings took great pride in the library. It was their goal to have a copy of every book ever written. They were not always fair in their efforts to obtain books for the library. King Ptolemy III confiscated books from all travelers whose ships stopped in the harbor. If he wanted the book for his collection, he kept it and returned a shoddily done copy to the original owner. He also refused to return copies of comedies that he had borrowed from the library in Athens.

The library itself was not like present-day libraries. The biggest difference was that the "books" were written on long papyrus scrolls. Papyrus is a type of reed that grows in the Nile River delta. The ancient Egyptians discovered that they could press these reeds into a smooth writing material that was fairly durable in their dry climate. Long sheets of papyrus were rolled up into scrolls. These scrolls did not stand up on shelves like books, but had to be stacked in cubbyholes or stored in buckets.

Scrolls were not as easy to read as our books with separate pages. The writing was done in columns and the reader unrolled the scroll sideways. Papyrus was so expensive that people often wrote notes in the margins of old texts and between the columns of writing, or they even wrote an unrelated book on the back of a scroll. The start of a scroll with the author's name on it was easily damaged. Librarians doing repair work sometimes glued fragments of rolls together or added the wrong beginning to a text. This made organizing and cataloging all the material in the library a difficult and demanding job.

Eratosthenes was promoted to chief librarian in 235 B.C. He soon made the most of being in charge of the best collection of books in the ancient world.

He was the first person to do a serious study of chronology, the science of arranging the order of events. This was not as easy a task as it might seem. There was no universal way of determining dates. Each city had its own method, often based on the rule of a particular king. Eratosthenes developed a more general chronology based on the Olympic Games. He divided time into groups of four years, called olympiads. He wrote a book on the Olympic victors and another one called *Chronography*. We still accept his dates for many events in ancient history.

Like many other scientists in ancient Greece, Eratosthenes knew that the world is round. The known world stretched from Spain in the west to India to the east. Eratosthenes thought that the rest of the sphere was covered by the Atlantic Ocean. He speculated that "If it were not that the vast extent of the Atlantic sea rendered it impossible, one might even sail from the coast of Spain to that of India along the same parallel."[5] This idea inspired the famous journey of Christopher Columbus many centuries later in 1492. Columbus, however, underestimated the size of the earth. He would have been better informed if he had consulted Eratosthenes' work on that point as well.

Eratosthenes figured out a brilliant way of calculating the size of the large sphere on which he stood. He knew that at noon on the longest day of the year in Syene (now Aswan), the sun's rays reached the bottom of a deep well. This meant that the sun was directly over Syene. Eratosthenes measured the angle of a shadow cast by a stick at noon on the same day in Alexandria, which was due north of Syene. He assumed that the rays of light from the sun are parallel. He measured the angle between the top of the stick and the end of its shadow. Then he divided that number into 360 (the number of degrees in a circle) to find out what fraction of a circle separated the two cities. The distance turned out to be one-fiftieth (1/50) of a circle.

Eratosthenes then hired a pacer to count off the exact distance between Alexandria and Syene. In those days, distances were measured by professional pacers who had been trained to take equal-sized steps. By multiplying that distance by fifty he calculated that the distance around the earth is 29,000 miles. The actual distance around the earth's polar circumference is approximately 24,900 miles. Eratosthenes' value is amazingly accurate, considering his methods for taking measurements. The theory behind his calculation is completely sound and is still used in modern calculations of the earth's size.

Eratosthenes combined mathematics and geography in another way. He was the first person to give maps a mathematical basis by using lines similar to the lines of latitude and longitude on current maps. He wrote a three-volume set of books called *Geography*. The three volumes covered the form and nature of the earth, his mathematical ideas, and a description of different countries and their politics.

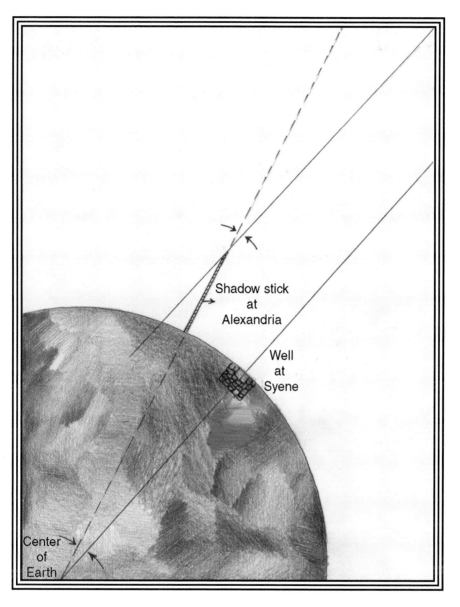

Eratosthenes devised a method for measuring the earth, using a shadow stick, a professional pacer, and mathematics.

Julius Caesar consulted these books a hundred years later when he conquered Europe.

Eratosthenes gathered information for his geography books from many different sources, piecing clues together like a detective. He read descriptions of places in history books. Sometimes the actual distances between cities were given in a measurement called stadia. Other times he had to guess the distance on the basis of the number of days it took to travel from one city to another. He could also guess the respective locations of places on the basis of similarities in the plants and animals that lived there or from a general description of the climate. Knowing which stars were visible from a particular city was another clue to its location. He could tell if places were on the same latitude from the length of their longest or shortest days.

Scale and grid are now considered essential parts of a map, but their significance was not appreciated at the time. Strabo, a great geographer and historian who lived two hundred years later, dismissed Eratosthenes as "a mathematician among geographers and a geographer among mathematicians."[6] He did not understand how important Eratosthenes' work would be in the field of navigation.

In spite of the people who belittled him, one of his most famous peers thought highly of him. Archimedes dedicated two of his works to Eratosthenes. One was a very complicated arithmetic problem. Eratosthenes' own mathematical work was as varied as the rest of his interests. He figured out a way to identify prime numbers (numbers that have only themselves and one as factors) now known as the sieve of Eratosthenes. He also studied the mathematical theory of musical scales.

Eratosthenes lived to be eighty years old. He served as chief librarian of the royal library of Alexandria under three kings. To show his respect for King Ptolemy III, he dedicated the solution of a famous math problem to him. The prince whom he had come to Alexandria to tutor later became King Ptolemy IV. Eratosthenes died during the reign of King Ptolemy V, Ptolemy III's grandson, in the year 194 B.C.

Pliny

6

Pliny

(A.D. 23–79)

Gaius Plinius Secundus, who is better known as
Pliny the Elder, wrote a thirty-seven volume
encyclopedia on the natural history of the world.
This was a big undertaking, but Pliny was equal to
the task. He was a man of great energy who needed
very little sleep. He was also a man of great curiosity.
In fact, it is fair to say that Pliny was doomed by his
scientific curiosity. He died near Mount Vesuvius on
August 25, A.D. 79, when he sailed too close to the
erupting volcano.

Pliny was born in the city of Como in northern
Italy some time around A.D. 23. Not much is known
about his childhood, not even the names of his parents. The family seems to have been well respected
and was probably quite wealthy.[1] At the age of

twelve, Pliny was sent to Rome, where he received a good education in literature, law, and oratory (the art of public speaking). After he finished school, Pliny became a cavalry officer in the Roman Army. He was posted to the German frontier, where he served with the future emperor Titus.

While on his travels, Pliny took a great interest in everything that related to the natural world. His first book, however, shows that he also paid attention to his work as an Army officer. The book was called *On Throwing the Javelin from Horseback.* He then wrote a longer book, titled *History of Rome's German Wars.* Unfortunately, copies of these books no longer exist; only their titles have survived.

After several postings, Pliny left the army in A.D. 58 and returned to Italy. For the next few years he lived quietly as a landowner, writing books on grammar and on the education of an orator. These may seem to be rather dull subjects, but this was a good time for Pliny to lie low. Nero was now in charge of the Roman Empire. According to Pliny's nephew, the later years of Nero's rule were a time when it was "dangerous to write anything at all independent or inspired."[2] Nero's reign was marked by violence from the start. He became emperor in A.D. 54, when his mother poisoned her husband, who was Nero's stepfather. A few years later, Nero murdered his mother and, after that, his wife. During his reign three quarters of Rome was destroyed by fire.

When Nero's rule ended with his suicide, he was succeeded by the emperor Vespasian. Pliny had known Vespasian's son Titus during his army days. He soon became good friends with the new emperor and held several government positions. He was put in charge of the empire's financial affairs in Spain, which gave him the chance to travel. In addition to going to Spain, he visited Gaul and North Africa. Pliny's official work did not take all his energy. He still found time to write. During this period, he completed a twenty-volume history of Rome.

Pliny never married. He adopted his sister's son—who was also named Pliny—as his heir. Pliny the Younger is the author of several books of letters and speeches. From the younger Pliny's letters, we learn that his uncle was blessed with a tremendous amount of energy. He used to get up at midnight and work until dawn. He was obsessed with gathering information. He had someone read to him while he was eating and bathing. Even when he was traveling, he read constantly and dictated notes to his secretary.

All this information resulted in *Natural History*, an encyclopedia on "the whole of nature."[3] *Natural History* is an important work because it sheds light on the thinking and culture of Pliny's time. It also brings together and preserves much of the knowledge that had been amassed in earlier times. Pliny's view of the natural world was very broad. He included far more than botany and zoology in his thirty-seven volume encyclopedia. The first book is an index of the topics covered in the other volumes. He states that 100 authors provided him with 20,000 important facts for his work, but the index mentions far more authors and observations—473 and 34,707, respectively. The second book covers the universe, ending with the earth. The next books cover geography, people, plants, animals, and medicine. The final volumes are about metals and stones, including their uses in medicine, architecture, and art.

Pliny was more of a collector of information than a real scientist. Most of his facts came from other writers, although he did include firsthand observations from his travels. His tour of duty in Spain provided him with original material. He was apparently impressed by the Spanish people. Comparing Spain and Gaul, he wrote that "Spain is superior . . . by reason of her incentive to toil, her schooling of slaves, and the hardiness of body and eagerness of heart displayed by her inhabitants."[4] He was, however, shocked by the Spanish way of mining gold, which destroyed whole mountainsides. Although Pliny does not rank as a great philosopher, in some ways his views were ahead of his time. He loved the natural world and felt that it was everyone's duty to preserve it. He insisted that as well as respecting large animals like elephants and lions, we should not overlook the perfection of the smallest insects.

Pliny was so focused on presenting information that he did not bother to separate facts from myths and legends. He summed up his approach by saying,

"Things must be recorded because they have been recorded."[5] After giving a correct account of how amber is formed, Pliny then goes on to list many strange superstitions associated with it. In his volume on animals, he includes a section on the behavior of dragons. It was believed that they attacked elephants and drank their blood. The dragons did not, however, live to benefit from their meal. Pliny states that:

> [the dragon] fixes its teeth behind the ear, that being the only place which the elephant cannot protect with the trunk. The dragons, it is said, are of such vast size that they can swallow the whole of the blood, consequently, the elephant being drained of its blood, falls to the ground, exhausted, while the dragon, intoxicated with the draught, is crushed beneath it and so shares its fate.[6]

Pliny completed *Natural History* in A.D. 77, just two years before his death. He dedicated it to his friend Titus. The work involved in producing the encyclopedia must have been staggering. Tens of thousands of bits of information written on scraps of papyrus had to be sorted into categories and finally into books. Pliny was rightfully proud of his achievement. In a preface to one volume he made the claim that until then "no Greek by himself had compiled an encyclopedia of the whole of nature; and no Roman had done so by himself or with others."[7]

At the time of his death, Pliny the Elder was commander of the fleet based at Misenum in the Bay of Naples. On the morning of August 24, A.D. 79 his nephew and his sister were visiting him. Over a distant mountain, they noticed a strange cloud shaped like a pine tree, with a tall trunk and spreading branches. They called Pliny away from his work to see it. He immediately ordered a vessel so that he could get a closer look.

After sailing through a rain of hot cinders, Pliny eventually arrived at Stabiae, where his friend Pomponius Mela lived. Pomponius had loaded most of his belongings into a boat and was ready to leave, but the strong onshore wind prevented him from setting sail. By this time it was evening, so Pliny, Pomponius, and their companions went up to the villa to pass the night. Only Pliny got any sleep. He was a heavy man and he snored rather loudly, but it was not his snoring that kept the others awake. The house was rocking on its foundations and pumice stones and cinders were falling on the roof. In the morning, everyone headed back down to the shore. The waves were so high that it was not possible to launch the boat. Still feeling tired, Pliny lay down on some sailcloth. He then asked his servants for a drink of water. When two of them went over to help him, they found he was dead.

Pliny the Younger, who had stayed behind in Misenum, gives a detailed account of his uncle's death. He wrote that Pliny "suffocated . . . by some gross and noxious vapor."[8] Since none of the others died, it is still a matter of debate whether Pliny

An artist's rendition of the eruption of Vesuvius in 79 A.D. While some historians maintain that Pliny died from a heart attack, others believe that poisonous gases from the volcano killed him.

suffocated from the volcanic gases or died of a heart attack. His extreme tiredness was out of character and may indicate that he was ill. Whatever the reason, his death in the shadow of an erupting volcano was a dramatic conclusion to the life of the author of a thirty-seven volume encyclopedia of the wonders of the natural world.

Galen

(A.D. 129–c. 199)

Galen was the most famous doctor in the Roman Empire. He practiced medicine in the tradition of the Greek doctor Hippocrates, who lived six hundred years before him. Galen, like Hippocrates, believed that people should eat a balanced diet, exercise regularly, and practice good hygiene. He studied and wrote commentaries on the work of earlier scientists in the fields of anatomy, physiology, and biology. He applied this knowledge to medicine and rose to the top of his profession. He was also the court physician to the emperor.

Although Galen was Greek, he spent much of his life in Rome. Almost three centuries earlier, the Roman Empire had expanded to take control of all the countries around the Mediterranean Sea, including

Galen

Greece. However, Greek culture and language did not suffer. Greek remained the language of science and philosophy. Latin was the language of government. Educated people throughout the empire were mostly bilingual, so Galen was able to communicate quite easily with his patients in Rome. In spite of being a foreigner, he was readily accepted.

As well as being a good doctor, Galen was a prolific writer. His books on anatomy and on medicine were used as the standard texts in medical schools for nearly fifteen hundred years. He wrote so many books that even he had a hard time remembering all of them. He finally listed his many titles in a book called *On the Arrangement of His Own Writings*. A large section of this book was devoted to his own education and philosophy. Because of this, we know more details about Galen's life than about the lives of the other ancient scientists.

Galen was born in A.D. 129 near the city of Pergamum in Asia Minor. His father, Nikon, was an architect and a wealthy landowner. As a young boy, Galen studied at home. When he was fourteen, he attended courses in philosophy, which gave him a well-rounded education. At sixteen, he decided to study medicine. This was the usual age to begin medical studies in those days. What was unusual was that within the next four years Galen wrote three books.

When Galen was twenty, he left Pergamum to continue his medical education in Corinth, Greece, and then in Alexandria in northern Egypt. At that time, the medical school in Alexandria led the world in the study of anatomy. The Egyptian practice of embalming corpses and making mummies had added a great deal to the knowledge of the human body. But Egyptian law forbade physicians to dissect corpses. However, for a short time about four hundred years earlier, the rulers of Egypt had supplied the medical school in Alexandria with the bodies of convicts.[1] Galen records that Herophilus and Erasistratus, who taught at the medical school during that era, performed the first recorded dissections on the human body.[2] Herophilus discovered that the arteries carried blood and not air, as was previously thought. He distinguished tendons from nerves and understood the anatomy of the eye. Erasistratus studied the brain and the nervous system.

By the time Galen enrolled at the medical school, dissecting corpses was again forbidden. He learned human anatomy by examining skeletons and studying the writings of Herophilus and Erasistratus. Their original texts have all been lost. Most of what we know about their ideas is from quotations in Galen's books. Galen also learned anatomy by dissecting animals. He examined everything from dogs and monkeys to at least one elephant.[3] Before the days of antiseptics and refrigeration, dissecting the corpse of an elephant was dangerous and smelly work. Galen ran a high risk of catching a deadly infection.

After studying medicine for twelve years, Galen returned to Pergamum and became the official doctor to the gladiators. Gladiator fighting was a popular spectator sport during the Roman Empire. Men, singly or in groups, fought to the death with swords while the crowds cheered the winners. The contestants were usually condemned criminals, prisoners of war, or slaves, although free men sometimes fought for glory or to pay off their debts. Gladiator fighting provided plenty of work for the doctors. Part of Galen's job was to take care of the health of the contestants before a fight. He supervised their diet and their exercise program. After the games he spent his time mending broken limbs and crushed skulls and binding deep cuts.

With so many open wounds to treat, it is not surprising that Galen became interested in the circulation of the blood. He thought that veins were on the right side of the body and that they carried blood to the heart. Arteries on the left side carried the blood away. He believed that the blood seeped into the heart and was sent to organs that needed it. He thought that air was drawn into the lungs to cool the blood. Although Galen's theories about the circulation of blood were mistaken, he was held in such great respect that his ideas were not challenged for hundreds of years. It was not until the seventeenth century that William Harvey, an English physician, came up with the correct theory. Harvey recognized that the heart is a pump that propels blood through

The Colosseum in Rome, now in ruins, was the scene of many gladiatorial contests.

the arteries and that the blood returns to the heart through veins.

In A.D. 161, war between the people of Pergamum and their neighbors, the Galatians, put an end to the games. Galen, who was now thirty-one, found himself without a job. He decided to go to Rome, where he rented a large house and opened a medical practice. He soon became a very successful doctor and cured many influential patients. He still had time for writing, though, and he also enjoyed attending lectures, particularly about philosophy.

Galen never married, and he does not seem to have had many close friends. One of the few people he mentioned by name was the philosopher Eudemus. When Eudemus became ill, Galen was invited to join the team of doctors who were treating him. He was soon involved in a violent quarrel over the correct treatment. Unfortunately, Galen had a short temper and was not afraid to speak his mind. Feelings ran so high that Galen was warned that his life was in danger. He decided it was time to return to Pergamum. Later, he gave a different reason for his hurried departure from Rome. An infectious disease was sweeping through the city. Galen wrote: "When the great plague broke out, I left the city and hastened home."[4] This does not seem to be the most noble reason for the greatest doctor in the Roman Empire to decide to leave his practice!

A few years later, Galen's skill in binding wounds was again in demand. He was ordered to join the

Roman legions who were fighting enemies on the northern frontier of the empire. Soon after he arrived, Emperor Marcus Aurelius sent him back to Rome to act as personal doctor to his eight-year-old son, Commodus. Galen looked after the boy's health for the next six years. Commodus was a husky lad with little need for a doctor, so Galen had plenty of time to continue writing.

Galen's second stay in Rome lasted twenty years. During this period he witnessed the end of the golden age of the Roman Empire. Marcus Aurelius was a great leader, but his son Commodus was neither a successful nor a popular emperor. He spent his time hunting wild beasts or putting on costly games instead of governing his people. He was a very strong man and looked on himself as the new Hercules. By the year A.D. 192, Commodus' outrageous behavior was creating turmoil not just in Rome but throughout the empire. When he appeared in the games as a gladiator, even his supporters were enraged. He was assassinated soon afterward. That same year a fire broke out on the Sacred Way and destroyed the library where some of Galen's books were stored. Galen decided he had had enough of Rome and returned to Pergamum. Little is known about his final years. He died at the age of seventy in A.D. 199.

Galen's fame continued to grow with the passing centuries. Many of his books were translated into Arabic and later into Latin. By this route they reached medieval Europe. Although Galen was born a pagan, he believed there was only one god and that this god had made every organ in the human body for a definite purpose. Galen knew little about Christianity, which was just emerging as a religion during his lifetime, but his philosophy coincided with Christian beliefs. His writings were adopted by later Christian thinkers. They remained the foundation for medical knowledge for fifteen hundred years, or about fifty generations. That is a very long time, especially when compared to the rapid advances in medicine in the last fifty years.

An 1886 engraving depicting Ptolemy.

Ptolemy

(A.D. c. 100–c. 170)

The scientists of the ancient world were fascinated by the movements of the sun, the moon, the planets, and the stars. They came up with many different theories to explain the changing patterns of the night sky. The most famous of those ancient theories was described by the Alexandrian astronomer Ptolemy in his book *Almagest*. His proofs were so complicated and so convincing that his ideas remained unchallenged for over a thousand years—even those ideas that were spectacularly wrong!

Claudius Ptolemaeus, commonly known as Ptolemy, was born around the year A.D. 100. Scholars in the Middle Ages were confused by his name. They thought that he must be related to the kings of Alexandria. It is more likely, though, that he was simply born in an Egyptian town named after one of those kings.[1] Later, Ptolemy moved to the city of Alexandria, where he did his major work.

Alexandria was well within the southern boundary of the Roman Empire, which by the second century A.D. had reached its peak and was no longer expanding. Ptolemy lived during the reigns of the emperors Hadrian and Antoninus. Hadrian built a wall across the middle of Britain to mark the empire's northern border. His successor, Antoninus, ruled during an unusually peaceful period. Ptolemy did not have the opportunity to tutor a great military leader or change the course of any wars, so he is not mentioned in the history books of that time. Most of what we know about him is from his own writing, where we learn more about his ideas than about his personal life.

Ptolemy's first work was his most famous. It was a thirteen-volume set of books on astronomy called *Syntaxis Mathematike*. The name means "mathematical treatise." Many years later it was translated into Arabic and called the *Almagest*, meaning "the greatest work." This is the name by which it is commonly known today. Ptolemy had lofty goals for his "greatest work." He wanted it to be a textbook of all astronomical knowledge that would allow people to calculate the positions of the sun, the moon, and the planets for any given time—past, present, or future.

To create his astronomy tables, Ptolemy needed accurate observations taken over as long a time span as possible. He personally observed the movement of the stars and planets over a sixteen-year period between April 5, A.D. 125, and February 2, A.D. 141.[2] He also relied on the observations and theories of earlier astronomers, going all the way back to records taken in 721 B.C. in Babylon.[3]

Ptolemy was aware of the many different ideas that had been put forward to explain the movements of the stars and planets. The Pythagoreans (fifth century B.C.) thought that the earth, sun, moon, and planets all revolved around a central fire, orbiting in perfect circles. Aristotle (384–322 B.C.) claimed that the earth was the center of the universe. Aristarchus of Samos (c. 270 B.C.) boldly proposed that the earth might be a planet in orbit around the sun. The astronomer with the greatest influence on Ptolemy's work was undoubtedly Hipparchus of Nicaea (c. 190–127 B.C.). Although they were separated by three hundred years, Ptolemy wrote about Hipparchus as if he were an older fellow scientist and collaborator.[4]

Hipparchus was the only other ancient Greek astronomer to make accurate observations of the night sky over a period of time. He recorded the locations of the planets and stars between September 147 B.C. and July 127 B.C. His observations were remarkably accurate, considering his tools and equipment. The invention of the telescope was still more than seventeen hundred years in the future. The ancient Greek concept of time was also a problem for astronomers. The ancient Greeks did not divide time into equal-length hours. The day was divided into twelve hours and the night was divided into twelve hours, so the length of an hour changed with the time of year. The best device for measuring time was a water clock. In spite of these difficulties, Hipparchus measured the length of a year to within 6.5 minutes of our modern value.[5] He recorded detailed information on 1,080 different stars and was the first person to classify stars by magnitude.

Hipparchus was among those who thought that the earth was the center of the universe. Ptolemy expanded on Hipparchus' view of the universe, and it came to be known as the Ptolemaic system. The *Almagest* quickly became the most respected book on astronomy. Scribes no longer bothered to make copies of Hipparchus' books, so his writings have all been lost. This makes it hard for scholars to know exactly how much he contributed to Ptolemy's work.

Ptolemy did not believe that the earth rotated on its axis. He argued that if it did, an object thrown into the air would be left behind as the earth spun away from under it. He thought that the sun, the moon, the planets, and a giant sphere that contained the stars all traveled in circular orbits around the stationary earth.

The five planets—Mercury, Venus, Mars, Jupiter, and Saturn—that were visible to the early astronomers presented a difficult problem. The word *planet*, meaning "wanderer," comes from the ancient

Greek description of the way planets move through the sky. From very early on they were recognized as being different from the stars because they were unpredictable. Instead of having the regular circular motion of the sun, moon, and stars, planets wandered about within a path known as the ecliptic. They seemed to speed up and slow down, and sometimes even to stop or move backward. We now know the reason is that we are not observing them from a stationary platform. The planet earth is also revolving around the sun.

Planets travel in a flattened circle, or ellipse. The belief that they had to move in perfect circles created a problem for the ancient astronomers. To account for the apparent wanderings of the planets, they had to develop a very complex system.

According to the Ptolemaic theory, each planet traveled around the earth in a circular path called the deferent. However, the planet did not stay directly on this path. Instead, it orbited around a point on the path of the deferent while it revolved around the earth. The smaller circle that the planet made was called the epicycle. Although not the first person to come up with this idea, Ptolemy managed to work out a mathematical formula to support it. His calculations were tremendously complicated. The mathematics behind a geocentric (earth-centered) theory are much more complex than those for a heliocentric (sun-centered) theory.

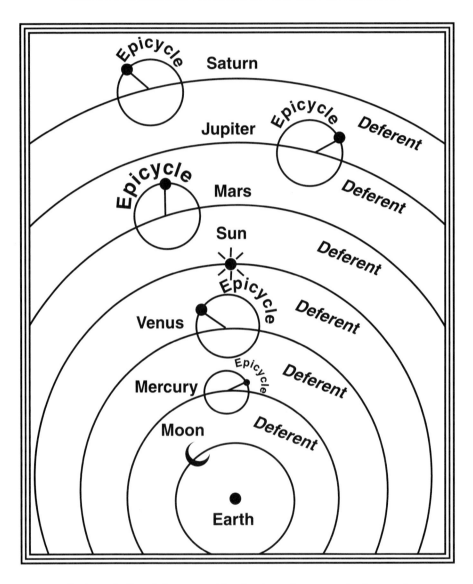

Ptolemy believed that everything in the universe revolved around the earth. This theory remained unchallenged for more than a thousand years.

Ptolemy wrote several other works relating to the heavens, including a set of tables called *Handy Tables*. He also wrote a set of four books on astrology called *Tetrabiblos*, which simply means "four books." In those days, this was the logical companion to a work on astronomy. One of the reasons early readers of the *Almagest* wanted to know the locations of planets was to determine the effect of the planets on their own lives. The first book of the *Tetrabiblos* discussed the benefits of forecasting from the stars. The second book covered the prediction of events such as natural catastrophes that affected everyone. The third and fourth books were on astrology as it related to individuals.

Ptolemy thought the planets could affect worldly events because they had different physical effects on the world. He thought that the moon increased moisture. Venus and Jupiter were connected with both heat and dampness, and Mars with heat and dryness. Saturn cooled and dried the world. Mercury's effect on heat and moisture depended on its relationship to the sun and moon. The exact location of a planet in the sky influenced the strength of its effect on the earth.

In a set of eight books called *Geography*, Ptolemy expanded on the work of Eratosthenes. The books contained mostly lists of latitudes and longitudes for various places but also included twenty-six maps. Much of the information came from merchants and soldiers, so it was not always accurate, especially for places beyond the Roman Empire.

Ptolemy died around A.D. 170. There is no account of his death, so it was probably a peaceful passing. The history of his memory is not as placid. The *Almagest* had a great influence on the course of astronomy. Everyone agrees about this, but what they cannot agree on is whether it was a good or a bad influence. Modern descriptions of Ptolemy's impact on astronomy reflect this turbulence. One fan of his work says, "[Ptolemy] combined an astounding power of synthesis and exposition with original genius."[6] Conversely, a critic states, "The *Syntaxis [Almagest]* has done more damage to astronomy than any other work ever written, and astronomy would be better off if it had never existed."[7] Ptolemy's writings were important because they promoted the study of astronomy. However, by being so thorough and so convincing, they kept scientists from forming more accurate theories about the movements of the planets. By having all the answers, Ptolemy stopped most people from asking questions for over a thousand years!

Hypatia

(A.D. c. 355–415)

Hypatia of Alexandria is one of the earliest known woman scientists. Although most accounts of Hypatia focus on her gruesome murder, she deserves to be remembered for what she did during her life. She was an accomplished mathematician, astronomer, and philosopher. She was also a wise and dedicated teacher. Romantic books have been written about her wisdom, her great beauty, and her tragic death. Recently, scholars have been trying to rediscover the real Hypatia.

Hypatia was born around A.D. 355 in Alexandria, Egypt.[1] At that time, Alexandria was the third largest city of the Roman Empire. Although some people claim that she studied in Athens, it is more likely that

An 1881 drawing depicting Hypatia.

she never left her native city.[2] She had no need to go anywhere else to complete her education.

From the time of its founding by Alexander the Great, Alexandria had been an important center of learning. It was a meeting place of the ideas of the Eastern and Western worlds. By the fourth century, the marble buildings were scarred by civil war and fire, but it was still a great city. Its location on the Mediterranean Sea made it an important naval base and a center for trade. The lighthouse of Pharos, one of the seven wonders of the ancient world, guarded its harbor.

The goal of the early kings of Alexandria was to have a library that contained copies of all the books in the world. Another important building for Alexandrian scholars was the Museum, or temple dedicated to the Muses. The Museum was a place where scholars could gather and exchange ideas. By Hypatia's time, the original Museum and the library buildings had been destroyed. The books were kept in the temple dedicated to Sarapis, the patron god of Alexandria. Sarapis was a combination of Greek and Egyptian gods that had been invented in an effort to unite the city in common worship.

Hypatia's father, Theon (A.D. c. 335–395), was a scholar at the Museum. He studied the writings of Euclid and Ptolemy and wrote poetry. He had high ambitions for his daughter. He wanted her to develop into "a perfect human being."[3] To reach this

These teachers felt at home in Alexandria, a center for learning.

goal, he taught her mathematics and astronomy. She seems to have been a willing student; she eventually surpassed her father in these subjects.

Theon wrote commentaries on the works of Euclid and Ptolemy. A commentary was like an updated edition of a book. Even in the dry climate of Egypt, books did not last forever. Over time the paper crumbled and the ink faded. Before the printing press, new copies of books—or rather, of scrolls—had to be made by hand. While doing this, scholars often revised the text. They made corrections and even added new material. Without these commentaries, important manuscripts would have been lost.

Hypatia also wrote commentaries. Unfortunately, we do not know exactly which ones. The only historical reference to her mathematical work states that "she wrote a Commentary on Diophantus, [one on] the astronomical Canon, and a Commentary on Apollonius's *Conics*."[4] Diophantus was the author of a thirteen-volume set called *Arithmetic*. Hypatia's version could be the one that has been passed down through the ages. The reference to the "astronomical Canon" is not clear. It may refer to Ptolemy's *Handy Tables*. It could also refer to Ptolemy's *Almagest*. A note in Theon's introduction to his commentary on the *Almagest* gives Hypatia credit for working on it with him.

In those days, it was rare for a girl or a young woman to receive a serious education. However,

Hypatia was not the only female scholar of ancient times. Eight hundred and fifty years earlier, Pythagoras included women in his community of philosophers. In ancient Greece, women looked after the sick and understood herbal remedies. Hippocrates looked favorably on their work, although he did not admit them to his school on the island of Cos. Then came Aristotle, who stated that women were inferior to men. His bias against women in science had long-lasting results. Pliny and Galen both refer to female doctors in the Roman Empire, but a woman mathematician or astronomer was very unusual.

Hypatia sometimes gave public lectures on mathematics and astronomy. These lectures were open to the upper classes, but she did not address the common people on street corners as many teachers did. She also taught philosophy to a select group of students. She taught a branch of philosophy called Neoplatonism. The exact details of her philosophy were shared only with the inner circle of her students. From what little we know, she stressed the perfection of the human soul through virtue, love of beauty, and intellectual discipline. Hypatia apparently practiced what she preached. She was greatly respected for her virtue and intelligence, and she dressed in simple clothing.

Hypatia was highly respected as a teacher. Her students attended lectures in her house. They came from all over Egypt and from as far away as Rome.

Many went on to hold powerful positions. Hypatia's students formed a close-knit group with strong ties to their teacher and to one another. Some of them corresponded with Hypatia for many years after they returned home. Most of what we know about Hypatia is from letters written to her by a student named Synesius. Unfortunately, her side of the correspondence was not preserved.

When Hypatia's students returned to their home cities, they continued to ask her advice. Many of them came back to visit. Her opinions were respected and acted upon. She also had practical skills and knew how to make scientific instruments. She gave her students instructions for making an astrolabe. The astrolabe was a complicated instrument that was used for measuring the altitude of the stars in relation to the horizon. In one of Synesius' letters, he asks her how to make a hydroscope, an instrument for measuring the weight of liquids. The letter was written in A.D. 413, the year of his death. He was in poor health at the time and was grieving the death of his three children. He wrote: "I am in such evil fortune that I need a hydroscope."[5] It is not clear what he wanted to do with the hydroscope. One suggestion is that he wanted it so that he could measure out his medicine.

Hypatia lived in Alexandria during a period of political and religious unrest. There was extensive fighting between Christians, Jews, and pagans in the city. (The term *pagan* covered everything from belief in the old Greek and Egyptian gods to following

Neoplatonic philosophy.) Conflicts between and within all these different religious groups often turned into bloody battles. People bragged about the number of opponents they killed. Although Hypatia was a pagan, her students included people with different beliefs. Two of them became Christian bishops.

The situation in Alexandria worsened when Theophilus became bishop in 385. He set about driving the pagans from the city and took over many of their temples for the church. The temple dedicated to Sarapis became a battleground. The statues to the gods were demolished and the scrolls from the library were burned. When Theophilus died in 412, his nephew Cyril became the new bishop. He was not a popular choice. He was power-hungry and wanted the church to take over many of the duties of the city government. This brought him up against the local governor, Orestes. Orestes was a Christian, but he was sympathetic to other religions.

Hypatia became a victim of the political turmoil. When she threw her support behind Orestes, Cyril became nervous. He was well aware that Hypatia could sway people with her words and that she had loyal students in important posts all over the empire. He was afraid to argue openly with Hypatia, so he and his supporters set about destroying her reputation. They planted rumors among the common people blaming her for the bloody conflict between the Christians and the Jews. They accused her of witchcraft and said that she practiced astrology and black magic. They claimed that "she beguiled many people through [her] satanic wiles."[6] They even accused her of putting a spell on Orestes so that he stopped attending church. Although Hypatia was highly respected by the upper classes, she was not a well-known figure among the common people, so the rumors took hold.

The smear campaign reached a dreadful climax one evening in March in the year 415. When Hypatia was coming home from a ride in the city, she was attacked by a mob led by a clergyman named Peter. The mob dragged Hypatia from her chariot and brutally murdered her. Then they burned her body in the street.

It has been suggested that the reason we know so little about Hypatia's life may be due to her violent death.[7] By the fifth century, most histories were written by Christian scholars. The death of such a wise and open-minded woman at the hands of a clergyman troubled them. It was easier to ignore Hypatia than to write about her.

A drawing depicting al-Khwārizmī, based on a nineteenth century portrait.

10

Al-Khwārizmī

(A.D. c. 780–c. 850)

Al-Khwārizmī was the mathematician who gave us the word *algebra* and introduced the idea of zero to the Western world. Historian George Sarton describes him as "one of the great scientists of his race and the greatest of his time. He [brought together] Greek and Hindu knowledge. He influenced mathematical thought to a greater extent than any other mediaeval writer."[1]

Although al-Khwārizmī lived closer to our own time than any of the other scientists in this book, scholars know very little about his personal life. From the dates on his mathematical writings, they guess that he was born some years before A.D. 800 and must have died after A.D. 847. His full name was Abu Ja'far Muhammad ibn Mūsā al-Khwārizmī.

This tells us that he was the son of Moses, the father of Ja'far and that he, or his ancestors, came from Khwarazm (now Khiva), a city that lies south of the Aral Sea in central Asia. Some historians say that he came from the district between the Tigris and Euphrates rivers.[2] He spent his adult life in Baghdad, which is now the capital of Iraq.

By the ninth century A.D., Arabia had emerged as a powerful country. With the collapse of the Roman Empire in the fourth and fifth centuries, Europe entered the Dark Age, the name given to the long period when education, art, and trade were neglected. Early in the seventh century the prophet Muhammad (570–632) founded the Muslim religion. The new religion spread through Syria, Palestine, and Egypt. It reached western Europe when Arab armies attacked and defeated the people of North Africa and then invaded Spain. The North African Muslims who conquered Spain are known as the Moors. The island of Sicily also came under Arab domination.

When al-Khwārizmī lived in Baghdad it was quite a new city, but its location at the meeting place of trade routes from India, Persia, and ports on the Mediterranean Sea had caused it to grow rapidly. From 813 to 823, Baghdad was ruled by the caliph (spiritual and political leader) al-Ma'mun. The caliph, who was himself an enthusiastic scholar and philosopher, soon turned the city into an important intellectual center.[3] He established the House of

The city of Baghdad, where al-Khwārizmī spent most of his adult life.

Wisdom and ordered his scholars to translate the classical Greek texts into Arabic. Copies of these books ended up in Muslim centers of learning in Spain and Sicily. Later, they were translated into Latin and passed on to universities throughout Europe. Without the work of the ninth-century Arab scholars, a great deal of earlier knowledge would have been lost forever.

Al-Khwārizmī was a member of the House of Wisdom, but he was more than just a translator. He wrote original books with new ideas that had a great impact in the field of mathematics. His most important work was a book on equations written in A.D. 820. The book is called *Al-jabr wa-al-muqabala,* which means "Completing and Balancing." The first word in the title gave us the term *algebra.*

In medieval Europe, the word *algebra* came to have wider meaning than just completing equations. Barbers were known as algebrists. This was not because they were especially good at mathematics but because, as a sideline, they often set broken bones, completing and reuniting them. They also practiced bloodletting. Today's candy-striped barber poles date back to the days when barbers wrapped bloody bandages around poles to attract business!

Al-Khwārizmī would probably have approved of this very practical meaning for the word *al-jabr.* He respected the need for mathematics in everyday life. Merchants had to be good at arithmetic so that they could add, subtract, and understand proportions.

Geometry was useful when it came to partitioning land. Algebra helped people solve problems connected with the complex Muslim laws of inheritance. The Greeks, on the other hand, were more interested in discovering the secrets of numbers than in using them. They studied the relationship between squares and triangles. They were fascinated by the ideas of prime numbers and parallel lines.

One of al-Khwārizmī's big breakthroughs came from studying the work of Indian mathematicians. In a book called *Addition and Subtraction by the Method of Calculation of the Hindus,* he introduced the idea of zero to the Western world. Several centuries earlier, some unknown Hindu scholar or merchant had wanted to record a number from his counting board. He used a dot to indicate a column with no beads, and called the dot *sunya,* which means empty. When the idea was adopted by the Arabs, they used the symbol "0" instead of a dot and called it *sifr.* This gave us our word *cipher.* Two hundred and fifty years later, the idea of *sifr* reached Italy, where it was called *zenero,* which became "zero" in English.

Using zero in combination with the Hindu symbols for one through nine (which are now known as Arabic numerals) made it possible to write any number, no matter how large, without inventing any more symbols. The new system was much more user-friendly than any of the earlier ones. Complicated fractions could now be expressed as decimals.

The previous Arabic number system had been similar to the Greek system. The Greeks used the twenty-four letters of their alphabet plus three other symbols. Those twenty-seven numerals were divided into three sets. The first set of nine corresponded to our numbers one through nine; the second set was for ten through ninety; the third set was for one hundred through nine hundred. Not only did the Greeks have to remember three times as many symbols as we do, but relations between numbers were harder to see.

When the new Arabic numerals were introduced into Europe, they replaced Roman numerals. The Roman system was a little easier than the Greek system because there were fewer symbols to remember, but it, too, was unwieldy. The Romans used the following letters to represent numbers:

$$I = 1 \qquad C = 100$$
$$V = 5 \qquad D = 500$$
$$X = 10 \qquad M = 1,000$$
$$L = 50$$

The numbers between one and one thousand are formed by combining and repeating these letters. Addition and subtraction are quite straightforward, especially on an abacus, or counting board. Multiplication and division are much more complicated.

The idea of zero as a symbol came before zero as a number. Zero, as a number, answers the question "How many?" It is, however, a strange number. Zero is the only number that can be divided by every other number, and the only number that can divide no other number. Understanding the properties of this new number, zero, became the test of a good mathematician. According to the writer Ali al-Daffaʾ, the Europeans did not appreciate the usefulness of zero right away. He states that "it took Europe at least two hundred and fifty years to accept and acknowledge the zero as a gift from the Muslims. . . . It was not until the late twelfth century that the Europeans really began to make use of the zero and the decimal system."[4]

Al-Khwārizmī did not limit his interests to mathematics. He wrote a book on geography called *The Book of the Form of the Earth*. The book contains lists of longitudes and latitudes for various cities, mountains, seas, islands, and rivers. He grouped places according to the amount of daylight on the longest day of the year. Some of his information came from Ptolemy's *Geography*, but al-Khwārizmī's book is more than just a translation of the earlier work. His world map is more accurate than Ptolemy's, particularly in areas that had been converted to the Muslim religion. He learned about places in Africa and the Far East from Arab merchants who had traveled to those distant countries.

Al-Khwārizmī also studied the stars. Caliph al-Maʾmun appointed him to the post of court astronomer. By way of thanks, al-Khwārizmī dedicated a book of tables describing the movements of the sun, the moon, and the planets to the caliph. The tables could be used for predicting eclipses of the moon and the sun. Some of the information came from records made in Baghdad, but al-Khwārizmī also drew on Hindu wisdom and on Ptolemy's tables. He used commentaries that had been made four centuries earlier by Theon and Hypatia of Alexandria.

In A.D. 842, al-Khwārizmī was ordered to go to Ephesus in Asia Minor by the new caliph, al-Wathiq, to investigate the tomb of the Seven Sleepers. Unfortunately, there are no details about what he learned on this exotic-sounding journey. The next mention of al-Khwārizmī is that he was one of a group of astronomers summoned to the caliph's sickbed in 847. On the basis of al-Wathiq's horoscope, the astronomers predicted that the caliph would live for another fifty years. He died ten days later.[5]

That is the last mention of al-Khwārizmī, the man who gave the world algebra and zero. He belongs with the great scientists of the ancient world not only because of his individual achievements but also because he represents a whole group of Muslim scholars. These ninth-century mathematicians gave us the decimal system and square and cube roots. They developed trigonometry and used the functions sine, cosine, and tangent. Another important contribution was that they kept science alive during the Middle Ages.

Chapter Notes

Chapter 1. Pythagoras

1. *Iamblichus: On the Pythagorean Life*, trans. Gillian Clark (Liverpool, England: Liverpool University Press, 1989), pp. 2–3.

2. George Sarton, *A History of Science*, vol. 1 (Cambridge, Mass.: Harvard University Press, 1952), p. 200.

3. Ibid.

4. *Iamblichus*, p. 8.

5. Ibid.

6. Kurt von Fritz, *The Dictionary of Scientific Biography*, vol. 11 (New York: Charles Scribner's Sons, 1975), p. 219.

7. J. B. Wilburand and H. J. Allen, eds., *The Worlds of the Early Greek Philosophers* (Buffalo: Prometheus Books, 1979), p. 83.

8. J. A. Philip, *Pythagoras and Early Pythagoreanism* (Toronto: University of Toronto Press, 1966), p. 200.

9. Sarton, p. 214.

10. Peter Gormon, *Pythagoras, a Life* (London: Routledge and Kegan Paul, 1979), p. 182.

Chapter 2. Hippocrates

1. George Sarton, *A History of Science*, vol. 1 (Cambridge, Mass.: Harvard University Press, 1952), p. 333.

2. Robert Joly, *The Dictionary of Scientific Biography*, vol. 6 (New York: Charles Scribner's Sons, 1972), p. 419.

3. Sarton, pp. 355–356.

4. David C. Lindberg, *The Beginnings of Western Science: The European Scientific Tradition in Philosophical, Religious, and Institutional Context, 600 B.C. to A.D. 1450* (Chicago: University of Chicago Press, 1992), p. 117.

5. Sarton, p. 345.

6. Joly, p. 419.

7. John Bartlett, *Familiar Quotations* (Boston: Little, Brown, 1980), p. 80.

Chapter 3. Aristotle

1. George Sarton, *A History of Science*, vol. 1 (Cambridge, Mass.: Harvard University Press, 1952), p. 470.

2. Paul Strathern, *Aristotle in 90 Minutes* (Chicago: Ivan R. Dee, 1996), p. 39.

3. Steve Parker, *Aristotle and Scientific Thought* (New York: Chelsea House Publishers, 1995), p. 19.

4. David C. Lindberg, *The Beginnings of Western Science: The European Scientific Tradition in Philosophical, Religious, and Institutional Context, 600 B.C. to A.D. 1450* (Chicago: University of Chicago Press, 1992), p. 64.

5. Sarton, p. 509.

6. Ibid., p. 473.

Chapter 4. Archimedes

1. E. J. Dijksterhuis, *Archimedes* (Copenhagen, Denmark: Ejnar Munksgaard, 1956), p. 12.

2. Ibid., p. 24.

3. Ibid., p. 19.

4. Ibid., p. 15.

5. *Greek Mathematical Works*, vol. 2, trans. Ivor Thomas (Cambridge, Mass.: Harvard University Press, 1941), p. 19.

6. Aubrey de Selincourt, *The War with Hannibal* (New York: Penguin Books, 1965), p. 338.

Chapter 5. Eratosthenes

1. George Sarton, *A History of Science*, vol. 2 (Cambridge, Mass.: Harvard University Press, 1959), p. 113.

2. D. R. Dick, *The Dictionary of Scientific Biography*, vol. 4 (New York: Charles Scribner's Sons, 1971), p. 389.

3. Sarton, p. 101.

4. Dick, p. 388.

5. E. H. Bunbury, *A History of Ancient Geography*, vol. 1 (New York: Dover Publications, 1959), p. 627.

6. Dick, p. 389.

Chapter 6. Pliny

1. David E. Eichholz, *The Dictionary of Scientific Biography*, vol. 11 (New York: Charles Scribner's Sons, 1975), p. 38.

2. Mary Beacon, *Roman Nature* (Oxford: Oxford University Press, 1992), p. 3.

3. Eichholz, p. 39.

4. Beacon, p. 4.

5. Eichholz, p. 39.

6. The editors of Time-Life Books, *Dragons* (Chicago: Time-Life Books, 1984), p. 23.

7. Eichholz, p. 39.

8. Raleigh Trevalyan, *The Shadow of Vesuvius* (Norwich, England: Jarrold and Sons, Ltd., 1976), p. 32.

Chapter 7. Galen

1. George Sarton, *A History of Science*, vol. 2 (Cambridge, Mass.: Harvard University Press, 1959), pp. 132–133.

2. Ibid., p. 130.

3. George Sarton, *Galen of Pergamon* (Kansas: University of Kansas Press, 1954), p. 41.

4. Leonard G. Wilson, *The Dictionary of Scientific Biography*, vol. 5 (New York: Charles Scribner's Sons, 1972), p. 230.

Chapter 8. Ptolemy

1. Olaf Pedersen, *A Survey of the Almagest* (Odense, Denmark: Odense University Press, 1974), p. 12.

2. Ibid.

3. Ibid., p. 408.

4. George Sarton, *A History of Science*, vol. 2 (Cambridge, Mass.: Harvard University Press, 1959), p. 286.

5. Lloyd Motz and Jefferson Hane Weaver, *The Story of Astronomy* (New York: Plenum Press, 1955), p. 46.

6. Sarton, p. 286.

7. Robert R. Newton, *The Crime of Claudius Ptolemy* (Baltimore: Johns Hopkins University Press, 1977), p. 379.

Chapter 9. Hypatia

1. Maria Dzielska, *Hypatia of Alexandria* (Cambridge, Mass.: Harvard University Press, 1995), p. 66. Some other sources give the date of Hypatia's birth as A.D. 370, but the dates of birth of some of her students make an earlier date more likely.

2. Ibid.

3. Margaret Alic, *Hypatia's Heritage* (Boston: Beacon Press, 1986), p. 42.

4. Michael A.B. Deakin, "Hypatia and her Mathematics," *The American Mathematical Monthly*, vol. 101, 1994, pp. 234–243.

5. Dzielska, p. 78.

6. Ibid., p. 91.

7. Ibid., p. 99.

Chapter 10. Al-Khwārizmī

1. George Sarton, *Introduction to the History of Science*, vol. 1 (Baltimore: Williams and Wilkins Company, 1927), p. 563.

2. G. J. Toomer, *The Dictionary of Scientific Biography*, vol. 7 (New York: Charles Scribner's Sons, 1973), p. 358.

3. Ali Abdullah al-Daffa', *The Muslim Contribution to Mathematics* (London: Croom Helm, 1977), p. 10.

4. Ibid., p. 37.

5. Toomer, p. 358.

Index